Graphic Organizers in Social Studies™

Learning About the American Revolution with Graphic Organizers

Linda Wirkner

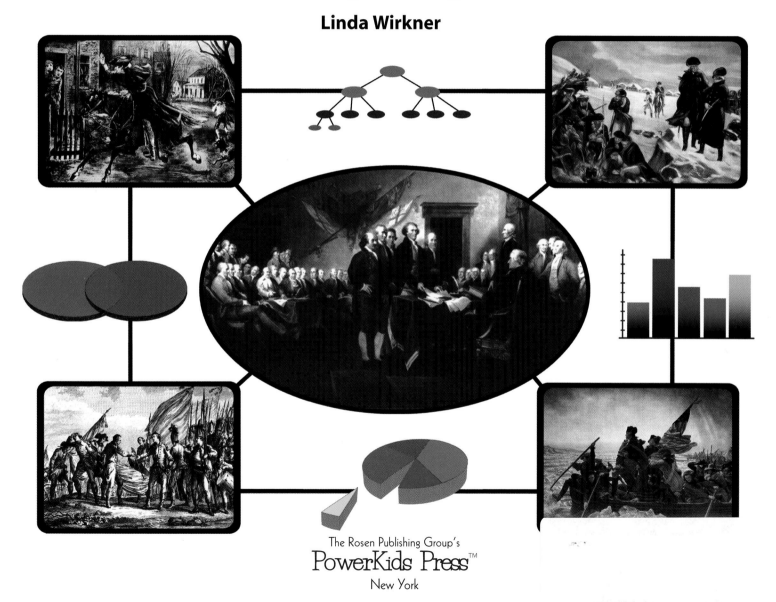

The Rosen Publishing Group's
PowerKids Press™
New York

To Michael with love

Published in 2005 by The Rosen Publishing Group, Inc.
29 East 21st Street, New York, NY 10010

Copyright © 2005 by The Rosen Publishing Group, Inc.

First Edition

Editor: Orli Zuravicky
Book Design: Michael Caroleo

Photo Credits: Cover and title page (middle), p. 12 (center middle, bottom middle, and bottom left) © Library of Congress Prints and Photographs Division; cover and title page (top left, top right and bottom right), pp. 8 (top left), 12 (top right), 15 (top left and bottom left) © Bettmann/CORBIS; cover and title page (bottom left), pp. 16 (top right and bottom right), 19 (bottom right) Dover Pictoral Archive Series; pp. 7, 11 (bottom left and bottom right), 19 (bottom left) © North Wind Pictures; p. 12 (top middle) © The Corcoran Gallery of Art/CORBIS; p. 12 (bottom right) © CORBIS; p. 20 © Superstock.

Library of Congress Cataloging-in-Publication Data
Wirkner, Linda.
Learning about the American Revolution with graphic organizers / Linda Wirkner.
   v. cm. — (Graphic organizers in social studies)
Includes bibliographical references and index.
Contents: The end of a war, the beginning of a revolution—Dividing the colonists—War breaks out—The Declaration of Independence—Leaders of the Revolution—War times—The war goes on—Joining the fight—The end of the Revolution—After the Revolution.
ISBN 1-4042-2813-6 (lib. bdg.) — ISBN 1-4042-5055-7 (pbk.)
1. United States—History—Revolution, 1775–1783—Juvenile literature. 2. Graphic organizers—Juvenile literature. 3. United States—History—Revolution, 1775–1783—Study and teaching (Elementary) [1. United States—History—Revolution, 1775–1783.] I. Title.

E208.W65 2005
973.3—dc22
                                        2003025068

Manufactured in the United States of America

M8368

Contents

Chart: Major Acts Passed by the British Government

Name of Act	Date Passed	Effect
Sugar Act	April 5, 1764	Placed a tax on sugar and molasses coming to colonies from non-British Caribbean islands.
Currency Act	April 19, 1764	Did not allow the colonists to make their own money.
Stamp Act	March 22, 1765	Placed a tax on legal papers, cards, newspapers, booklets, and other printed items in the colonies.
Quartering Act	March 24, 1765	Forced colonists to house British soldiers and offer them food and whatever else they needed.
Declaratory Act	March 18, 1766	Stated that the British government had the power to pass laws in the colonies and to force the colonists to follow those laws.
Townshend Acts	June 29, 1767	Placed more taxes on the colonies in a series of four acts. The most well known act placed a tax on tea, glass, lead, paints, and paper brought into the colonies.
Coercive, or Intolerable Acts	March 31, 1774	Closed Boston's port, did not allow any shipping or trade with Quebec, and made Massachusetts a royal colony instead of allowing it to remain self-governing. Protected British officers from being charged with any wrongdoing by the colonial governments.

The End of One War, the Beginning of Another

While the colonies were growing, England was fighting a war with France over which country would control America. In 1763, England won the war. To pay off its war **debt**, England taxed the colonies. Laws like the Townshend Acts taxed items such as paper and tea. The taxes angered colonists because they had no voice in the government that was taxing them. Boston colonists **protested** by dumping 342 chests of tea into the harbor on December 16, 1773. This event was called the Boston Tea Party. Colonists shouted, "No taxation without **representation**." In **response** to the Boston Tea Party, England passed the Intolerable Acts. Boston's port was closed and the number of British soldiers in the colonies increased. **Graphic organizers** are tools that can be used to help arrange and group different facts. This book will use graphic organizers to explain the American **Revolution**.

This graphic organizer is a chart. It lists different subjects in the left column. Facts about each subject appear in the columns to the right. This chart shows the major acts passed by the British government, when they were passed, and the effect of each act.

Dividing the Colonists

The Intolerable Acts angered the colonists, and they decided to get together and take action. A total of 56 **colonial** representatives met in Philadelphia for the First Continental Congress in September 1774. They sent an official letter of protest to George III, king of England. They also agreed to stop buying British goods. As the struggle between the colonies and England grew, so did disagreements between friends and family. Some colonists were called **loyalists** because they sided with the king. Other colonists wanted England and the colonies to come to an agreement. Many colonists became **patriots**, which means they wanted a complete separation from England. Patrick Henry, a famous patriot, spoke out against England. In a 1775 meeting of Virginia's government, Patrick Henry spoke the words, "Give me liberty or give me death." These were words of revolution.

The graphic organizer to the right is a compare/contrast chart. It shows two different points of view on several connected subjects. In this chart, the left column shows the subjects, and the other columns show the loyalists' and patriots' views on each subject.

Compare/Contrast Chart: Loyalist and Patriot Beliefs

	Loyalists	Patriots
The King	• The king is trying his best to run the colonies and England. He is not a bad person or ruler.	• The king is a bad person who is not honest. • A government run by a king does not work.
England	• The colonies need England to protect them from other countries and wars. • England is like family. We all came from the same place and we should not fight each other. • England's laws are trying to keep the colonies in order and have done more good than bad.	• England's government does not care about the colonies. It only cares about England. • England does not have the right to make laws for the colonies. • England does not have the right to tax the colonies. • England's government is not fair. Representatives buy and sell their seats. They are not elected fairly by the people.
The Colonies	• The colonies are not strong enough to succeed without England's help. • The colonies are not able to govern themselves. • The colonies should pay taxes to England because England has given the colonists so much and it is only fair that they should pay some of it back.	• Colonists have the right of representation in the government that is making their laws. • People have god-given rights of freedom. Colonists should be allowed to speak, print newspapers, and gather in peace whenever they want without British officers telling them that they cannot. • Colonial government will be better than England's government because the representatives will be fairly elected by the people and they will care about their country.

This is a hand-colored woodcut of Patrick Henry giving his famous "give me liberty or give me death" speech. He gave this speech on March 23, 1775. It took place at St. John's Church, during a meeting of Virginia's colonial government.

Sequence Chart: Paul Revere's Ride

April 18, 1775 – Around 10:00 P.M.
Paul Revere is told to ride to Lexington to warn Samuel Adams and John Hancock, famous patriots, that British troops are marching to arrest them. Revere leaves Boston.

↓

April 18, 1775 – Around 11:00 P.M.
Revere crosses the Charles River into Charlestown. There he starts his horseback ride to Lexington.

↓

April 19, 1775 – Around 12:00 A.M.
Revere arrives at Lexington and delivers his message to Hancock and Adams. Shortly afterward he meets up with William Dawes, another messenger, who joins him.

↓

April 19, 1775 – Around 12:30 A.M.
Dr. Samuel Prescott joins Revere and Dawes. The three ride off to Concord together, spreading the word about the British troops.

↓

April 19, 1775 – Around 1:00 A.M.
Revere, Dawes, and Prescott meet British soldiers. The British soldiers capture the three men, but Dawes and Prescott escape. Revere is held as a prisoner.

↓

April 19, 1775 – Between 2:00 and 5:00 A.M.
Revere is let go. He rides back toward Lexington. He helps Adams and Hancock escape the British soldiers. By this time, minutemen have gathered and begin marching toward Lexington. The British soldiers and minutemen meet. Shots are fired and the American Revolution begins.

Paul Revere was a famous silversmith in the colonies. He was also a patriot. Here he is riding through colonial towns warning the colonists and the minutemen that the British are coming.

War Breaks Out

The king sent hundreds of British soldiers to the colonies to control the colonists. Colonists began to form small armies, called militias, to guard themselves. Minutemen were militia soldiers who were ready to fight at a moment's notice. In April 1775, a British general sent 700 soldiers to Concord, Massachusetts, to steal the colonists' **weapons** and arrest two colonial leaders. Paul Revere, a messenger, was sent to spread the word about the British plan. He and two other men rode all night shouting that British soldiers were coming. When they reached Lexington, Massachusetts, on April 19, the minutemen and other militia stood ready to fight. Shots were fired and eight colonists were killed. The American Revolution had begun. In May, the Second Continental Congress met in Philadelphia and created a **Continental army**. They appointed George Washington to be its commander.

This graphic organizer is a sequence chart. It arranges the order of different events or steps in a process from start to finish. This sequence chart shows the order of events of Paul Revere's ride, and that of the other messengers, the night before the Battle of Lexington and Concord.

The Declaration of Independence

Early battles were costly for both sides. On June 17, 1775, British and American troops fought at Bunker Hill. Although the British won the battle, they lost more than 1,000 soldiers. Later in 1775, the Battle of Quebec left many Americans dead. Despite the fighting, the colonies were not officially free from English control, and colonists remained **divided** on the subject. In January 1776, Thomas Paine wrote a paper in favor of independence called *Common Sense*, which changed people's minds in favor of independence. In June, Congress appointed a group of men to write a **declaration** of freedom. On July 4, 1776, Congress adopted the Declaration of Independence. Messengers carried copies of it to towns throughout the colonies. George Washington read the declaration aloud to the first soldiers of the United States.

The graphic organizer to the right is a KWL chart. This KWL chart tells the basic facts about the American Revolution. The first column lists basic facts that you already know about the Revolution. The next column lists questions about each fact that you might want to know, and the last column uses what you've learned in the chapter to answer those questions.

KWL Chart: The Beginning of the Revolution

What I Know	What I Want to Know	What I've Learned
• Colonists were angry about how England had been treating them. They were angry about the taxes that were being passed, and they wanted to have representatives in their government.	• Did all of the colonists feel the same way?	• Some colonists were in favor of independence and some were not. Patriotic papers, such as *Common Sense*, were written and handed out in the colonies to try to make loyalists change their minds in favor of independence.
• In the mid 1770s, colonies formed small armies just in case they had to guard themselves from British soldiers.	• Did the colonies have an official army?	• During the Second Continental Congress, which met in 1775, a colonial army was created. They named it the Continental army, and it was commanded by George Washington.
• By 1775, battles had broken out between some British soldiers and colonists at Lexington and Concord, at Bunker Hill, and in Quebec.	• When did the colonies officially break away from England?	• The Declaration of Independence was signed on July 4, 1776. The colonies officially declared themselves independent from England. They would have to win the war for England to recognize their freedom, though.

This painting shows the Battle of Bunker Hill. British soldiers were called redcoats because of the red color of their army coats.

Artist James Wright created this hand-colored engraving of General George Washington.

Concept Web: The Framers of the Declaration of Independence

Benjamin Franklin was born in 1706. He was a representative from Pennsylvania. He was an inventor, a scientist, and a patriot. Franklin was a member of the Second Continental Congress and one of the writers of the Declaration of Independence.

Robert R. Livingston was born in 1746. He was a representative from New York and was a member of the Second Continental Congress. He helped to write the Declaration of Independence, as well as the New York State Constitution.

Thomas Jefferson was born in 1743. He was a representative from Virginia. He was a member of the Second Continental Congress. He was appointed to head the group of writers of the Declaration of Independence, and he wrote the first draft. He was the third president of the United States.

The Framers of the Declaration of Independence

John Adams was born in 1735. He was a representative from Massachusetts. He was present at both the First and Second Continental Congresses. It is said that he was the person who suggested that George Washington should command the army. He helped to write the Declaration of Independence. He was also a vice president and a president of the United States.

Roger Sherman was born in 1721. He was a representative from Connecticut. He was a member of the First and Second Continental Congresses. He, too, was a framer of the declaration.

12

Leaders of the Revolution

The leaders of the American Revolution were brave. If they won the war, they would be the founders of a new country. If England won, they would be seen as **traitors**. One important revolutionary leader was George Washington. As the commander of the Continental army, he gained respect and praise for being strong but caring. Washington was a smart and powerful leader. He was so **influential** that he was called the father of his country. Thomas Jefferson, another leader who shaped the new nation, was the main author of the Declaration of Independence. Another important leader, John Adams, was a member of both the First and Second Continental Congresses. He was **passionate** about independence. He wrote and spoke against England's taxes and laws. He helped to draft the Declaration of Independence.

This graphic organizer is a concept web. It shows one main idea in the center. Several other connected ideas are written in the boxes around the main idea. Concept webs tell facts about the main subject and show pictures of people or events that are connected to that subject. This concept web is about the framers, or writers, of the Declaration of Independence.

War Times

When King George III learned about the Declaration of Independence, he sent British troops to New York to take back the colonies. On September 15, 1776, 30,000 trained British soldiers entered New York City and took over. Continental troops were forced out of New York as well. On Christmas Day 1776, Washington and his men crossed the Delaware River into Trenton, New Jersey. They attacked British troops the next day. Fighting usually stopped for the winter, so the attack surprised the British and they quickly **surrendered**. In December 1777, Washington and his men spent the winter at Valley Forge, Pennsylvania. They did not have enough supplies or food to last through winter. Often soldiers had no shoes or shirts. Many men suffered from **frostbite** during that snowy winter. Sickness spread throughout the camp. Around 2,000 American soldiers died at Valley Forge.

This graphic organizer is a line graph. Line graphs can help show the change in something over time. This graph shows the change in the number of Continental soldiers from 1775 to 1783. These numbers are just estimates, which are good guesses. Notice how low the number drops in 1781.

Line Graph: Estimates of Numbers of Continental Soldiers 1775–1783

Below: In this painting of George Washington and his troops at Valley Forge, Pennsylvania, soldiers are gathered around a fire to stay warm.

Below: This painting is of Washington and his men crossing the Delaware River before the Battle of Trenton on the night of Christmas Day.

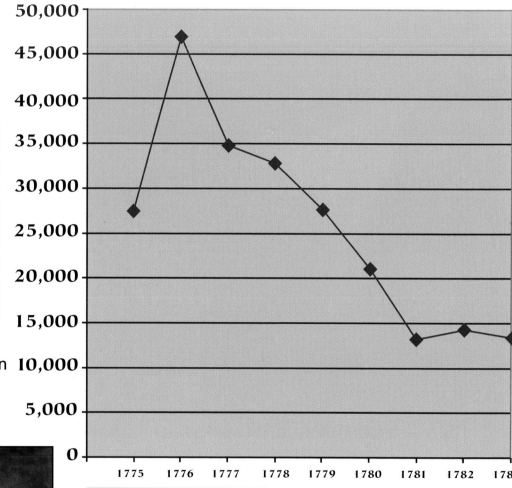

Year	Number of Soldiers
1775	27,443
1776	46,891
1777	34,820
1778	32,899
1779	27,699
1780	21,015
1781	13,292
1782	14,256
1783	13,476

Continental Soldiers

Map: Major Battles of the American Revolution and Who "Won" Them

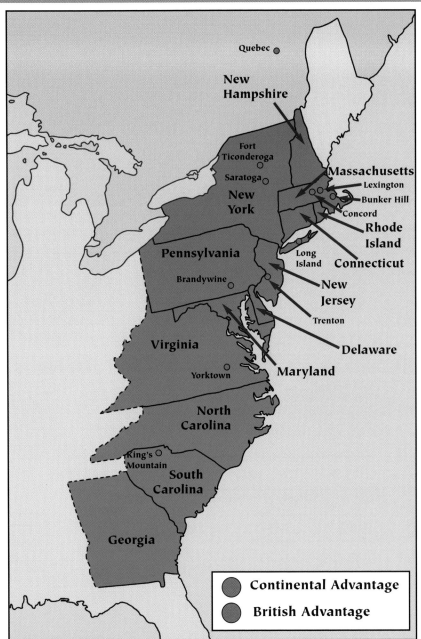

Quebec

New Hampshire

Fort Ticonderoga

Saratoga

New York

Massachusetts

Lexington

Bunker Hill

Concord

Rhode Island

Pennsylvania

Long Island

Connecticut

Brandywine

New Jersey

Trenton

Virginia

Delaware

Maryland

Yorktown

North Carolina

King's Mountain

South Carolina

Georgia

●	Continental Advantage
●	British Advantage

At the Battle of Saratoga, the Continental army lost 150 men. Six hundred British men were lost to death or wounds.

On October 17, 1777, at 2:00 P.M., the British officially surrendered to the Americans.

The War Goes On

The Continental army had little in common with the British soldiers. Washington's troops consisted of tradesmen, farmers, freedmen, and slaves. They lacked weapons and training. England, on the other hand, was known throughout Europe for its excellent army. Their soldiers were fully trained. They knew how to succeed in a battle. However, the Continental army fought hard. In the fall of 1777, Americans forced around 6,000 British soldiers to surrender in Saratoga, New York. After months of **ignoring** America's cry for help, France finally entered the American Revolution and fought on the American side. The **victory** at Saratoga had shown France that Americans were strong enough to fight England. France sent troops to America and gave money to the Continental army for guns and other supplies.

This map shows the major locations of the battles of the American Revolution. War battles were not always won. However, in every battle, one side came away with the advantage. This means that they left the battle in better condition than did the other side. The key shows which battles were British advantages and which were Continental advantages.

Joining the Fight

During the war, both armies needed more soldiers. The British hired German soldiers, called Hessians, and promised freedom to **enslaved** blacks after the war if they joined the fight. The Continental army also offered freedom to northern slaves who joined the American side. About 5,000 enslaved and free black men fought on both sides. Native Americans fought on both sides, too. However, most Native Americans fought for the British in hopes that they would stop the Americans from taking over more land. During battles, families often moved from one place to another, following their family members who were fighting. Women were cooks, nurses, and general aids. They carried water and **ammunition** to soldiers during battle. Sometimes they even took their husbands' places in battle if they died. A few women, such as Deborah Samson, dressed up as men to fight.

This graphic organizer is a classifying web. It organizes people or subjects into different groups based on certain common facts about them. This classifying web shows what kinds of people fought for each army and gives an example of a famous person from that group.

Classifying Web: Who Joined the Fight?

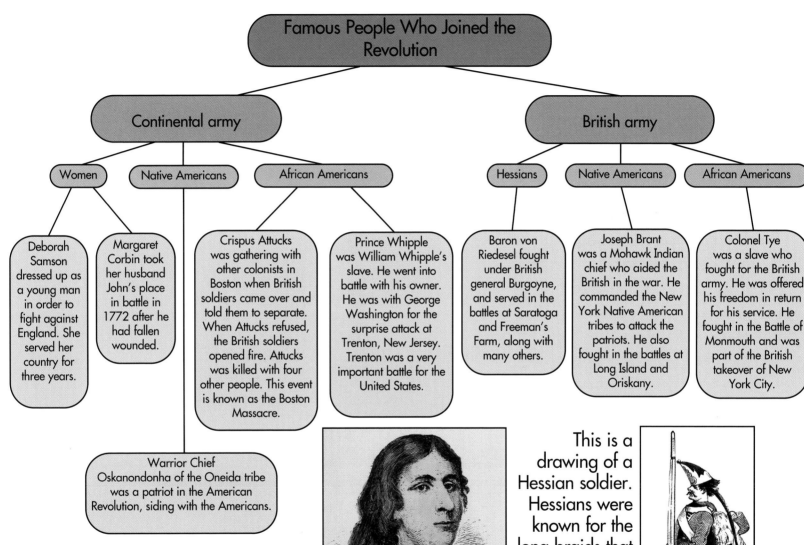

Famous People Who Joined the Revolution

Continental army

Women

Deborah Samson dressed up as a young man in order to fight against England. She served her country for three years.

Margaret Corbin took her husband John's place in battle in 1772 after he had fallen wounded.

Native Americans

Warrior Chief Oskanondonha of the Oneida tribe was a patriot in the American Revolution, siding with the Americans.

African Americans

Crispus Attucks was gathering with other colonists in Boston when British soldiers came over and told them to separate. When Attucks refused, the British soldiers opened fire. Attucks was killed with four other people. This event is known as the Boston Massacre.

Prince Whipple was William Whipple's slave. He went into battle with his owner. He was with George Washington for the surprise attack at Trenton, New Jersey. Trenton was a very important battle for the United States.

British army

Hessians

Baron von Riedesel fought under British general Burgoyne, and served in the battles at Saratoga and Freeman's Farm, along with many others.

Native Americans

Joseph Brant was a Mohawk Indian chief who aided the British in the war. He commanded the New York Native American tribes to attack the patriots. He also fought in the battles at Long Island and Oriskany.

African Americans

Colonel Tye was a slave who fought for the British army. He was offered his freedom in return for his service. He fought in the Battle of Monmouth and was part of the British takeover of New York City.

This is a hand-colored woodcut of Deborah Samson, who fought in the American Revolution. Her alias, or fake name, was Robert Shirtliffe.

This is a drawing of a Hessian soldier. Hessians were known for the long braids that they wore at the back of their heads.

19

Bar Graph: Casualties of the Battle of Yorktown

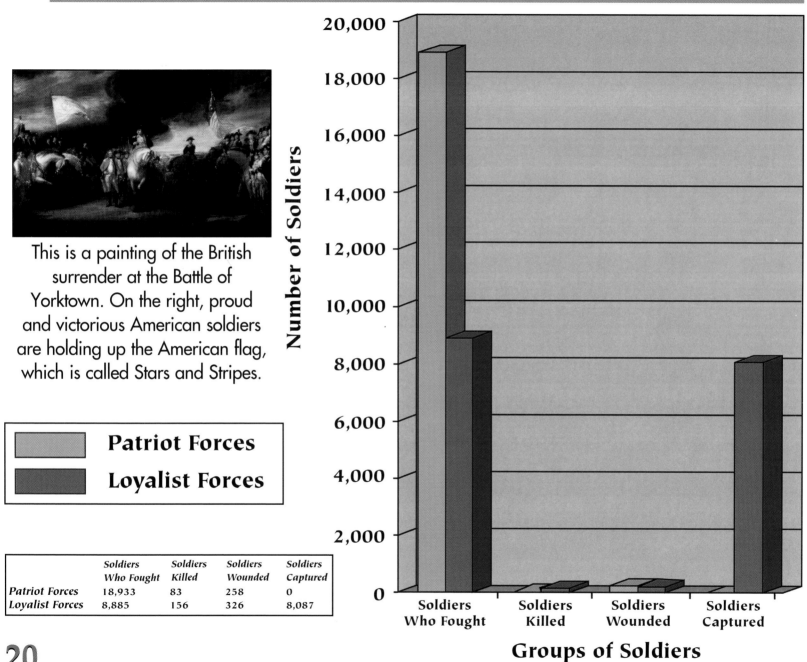

This is a painting of the British surrender at the Battle of Yorktown. On the right, proud and victorious American soldiers are holding up the American flag, which is called Stars and Stripes.

Patriot Forces

Loyalist Forces

Number of Soldiers

Groups of Soldiers

	Soldiers Who Fought	Soldiers Killed	Soldiers Wounded	Soldiers Captured
Patriot Forces	18,933	83	258	0
Loyalist Forces	8,885	156	326	8,087

The End of the Revolution

After Saratoga, it seemed that America was on its way to winning the war. However, in May 1779, America almost suffered greatly because of a traitor named Benedict Arnold. One of Washington's finest officers, Arnold had secretly planned to tell American secrets to the British. Luckily, Arnold was caught.

In the summer of 1781, Washington and his troops traveled for 500 miles (804.5 km) from New York City to Yorktown, Virginia, where British troops were camped. French ships also headed there. The American and French armies attacked Yorktown. The British commander was trapped. He surrendered on October 19, 1781. America had won the war. In 1783, eight years after the first battle at Lexington, the **Treaty** of Paris was signed. The United States was officially free of England's rule. The Revolution was over.

Bar graphs are used to show how things change over a period of time or how they compare to one another. This graph shows the number of casualties for both the British and Continental armies during the Battle of Yorktown. A casualty is a soldier who was wounded or killed in battle.

After the Revolution

The American Revolution cost the Americans 25,000 lives. It tore apart families, destroyed homes and farms, and divided the colonies. Loyalists no longer felt comfortable or welcome in their communities. About 100,000 loyalists returned to England or moved to Canada or other places after the war ended. Many of the Hessians who had fought for the British chose to remain in America and make new homes for themselves. General Washington thanked his men for their strength and belief in the fight for independence. When the last of the British forces left Philadelphia, citizens of the United States celebrated with fireworks. After eight years of battles, death, hunger, sickness, and **exhaustion**, soldiers finally went home to rebuild their lives and their families. The British suffered a great loss. For the Americans, this victory was the beginning of a new life.

Glossary

ammunition (am-yoo-NIH-shun) Things fired from weapons, such as bullets.

colonial (kuh-LOH-nee-ul) Having to do with the period of time when the United States was made of thirteen colonies ruled by England.

Continental army (kon-tin-EN-tul AR-mee) The name of the American army during the American Revolution.

debt (DET) Something owed.

declaration (deh-kluh-RAY-shun) Announcement.

divided (dih-VYD-ed) Separated.

enslaved (en-SLAYVD) The condition of being a slave.

exhaustion (ig-ZOS-chen) Being tired out.

frostbite (FROST-byt) Harm to the body caused by freezing.

graphic organizers (GRA-fik OR-guh-ny-zerz) Charts, graphs, and pictures that sort facts and ideas and make them clear.

ignoring (ig-NOR-ing) Paying no attention to something.

influential (in-floo-EN-shul) Able to sway one's opinion or point of view, having a big effect.

loyalists (LOY-uh-lists) People who are faithful to a certain political party, government, or ruler.

passionate (PA-shuh-nit) Feeling strongly about something.

patriots (PAY-tree-uts) People who love and defend their country.

protested (PROH-test-ed) To have acted in disagreement.

representation (reh-prih-zen-TAY-shun) The act of speaking on behalf of a person or a group of people.

response (rih-SPONS) Answer.

revolution (reh-vuh-LOO-shun) A complete change in government.

surrendered (suh-REN-derd) Gave up.

traitors (TRAY-turz) People who turn against their country.

treaty (TREE-tee) An official agreement, signed and agreed upon by each party.

victory (VIK-tuh-ree) The winning of a battle or a contest.

weapons (WEH-punz) Objects or tools used to injure, disable, or kill.

Index

A
Adams, John, 13
Arnold, Benedict, 21

B
Battle of Quebec, 10
Boston Tea Party, 5

C
Common Sense, 10
Continental army, 9, 13, 17–18

D
Declaration of Independence,
    10, 13–14

F
First Continental Congress, 6

G
George III, king of England, 6,
    14

H
Henry, Patrick, 6
Hessians, 18, 22

I
Intolerable Acts, 5–6

J
Jefferson, Thomas, 13

L
loyalists, 6, 22

M
minutemen, 9

N
Native Americans, 18

P
Paine, Thomas, 10
patriots, 6

R
Revere, Paul, 9

S
Samson, Deborah, 18
Second Continental Congress,
    9, 13

T
Townshend Acts. *See* Intolerable
    Acts.
Treaty of Paris, 21

W
Washington, George, 9–10,
    13–14

Web Sites

Due to the changing nature of Internet links, PowerKids Press has developed an online list of Web sites related to the subject of this book. This site is updated regularly. Please use this link to access the list:

www.powerkidslinks.com/goss/amrevgo/